WHAT SHOULD DANNY DO?

A DAY FULL OF CHOICES AND ADVENTURES

Danny was a little boy with big dreams. He didn't just want to be a superhero he believed he was one. His red cape swished behind him wherever he went. One bright morning, Danny woke up with a smile. "Today is my chance to prove I'm a real hero!" he said. But when he raced downstairs, his little brother tripped, spilling milk all over Danny's prized cape.

Danny froze. His fists clenched. What should Danny do?

Danny had two choices:

1. Yell, "Look what you've done!"

2. Help his brother clean the mess.

Danny took a deep breath. He chose to help. "It's okay," he said. Grabbing a towel, he wiped his cape and helped his brother clean the table. Mom, watching from the kitchen, smiled. "That's what real superheroes do," she said. Danny's heart swelled. Maybe he was a hero.

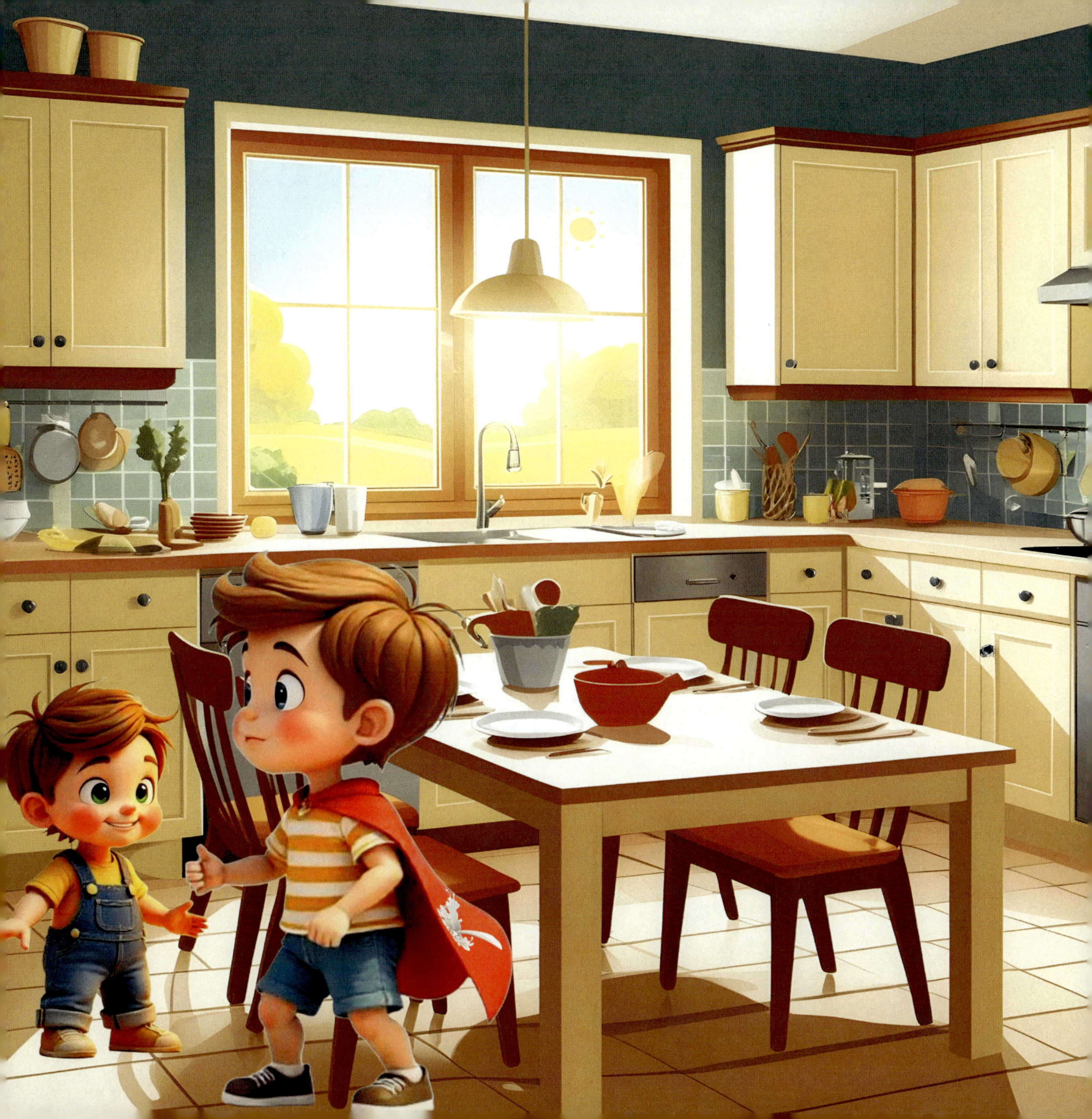

After breakfast, Danny bolted outside. His best friend, Sam, was waiting with a shiny new soccer ball. "Let's see your super-kick!" Sam challenged. Danny grinned and charged, aiming for a powerful shot. But he slipped, crashing into Sam. Both boys tumbled to the ground, the soccer ball rolling away.

Danny's cheeks burned. What should Danny do?

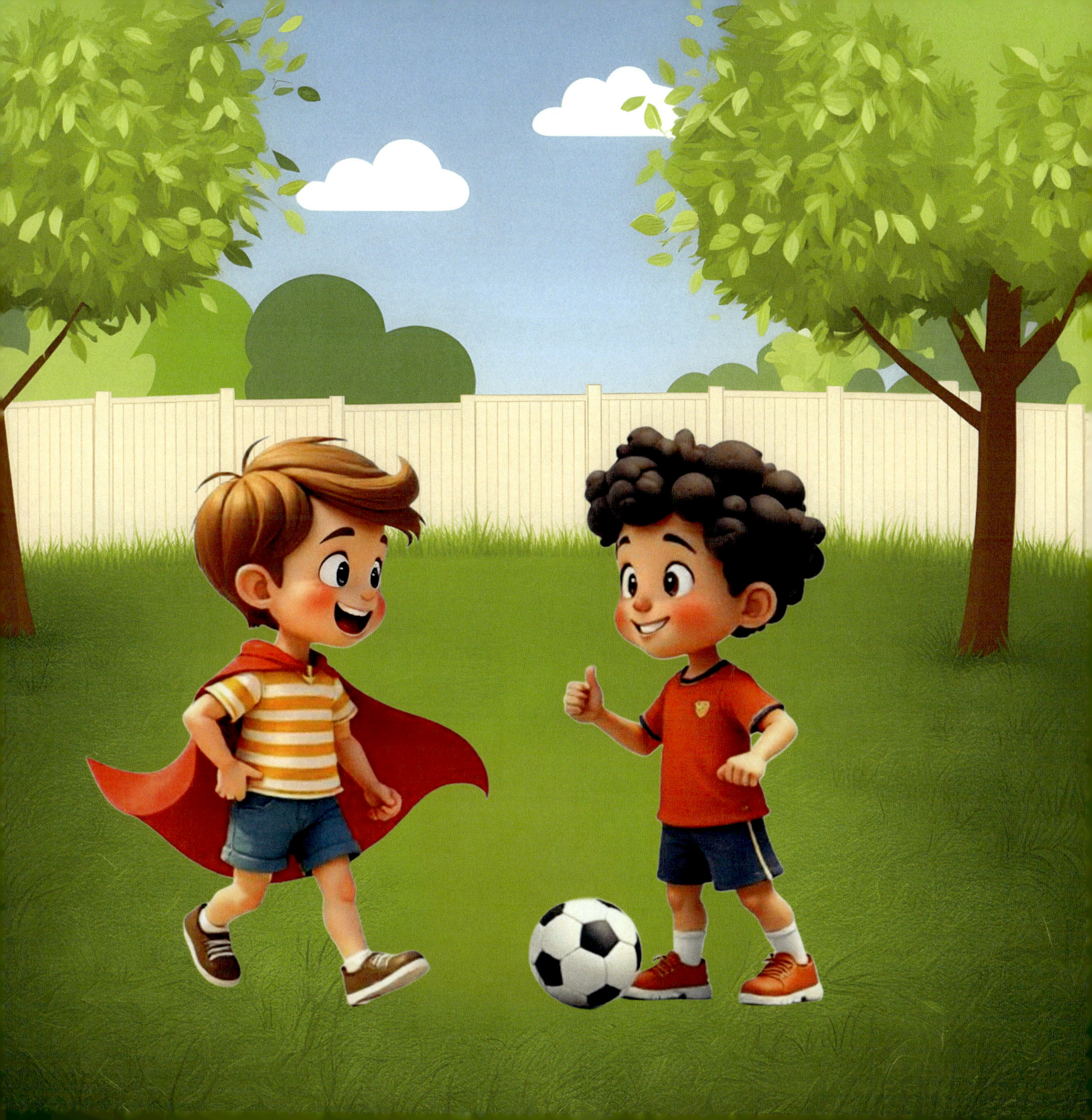

Danny had two choices:

1. Laugh it off and blame Sam.

2. Apologize and help him up.

Danny reached out his hand. "Sorry, Sam! Are you okay?" Sam dusted himself off and grinned. "No big deal! Let's try again." They kicked the ball back and forth until the whole yard echoed with laughter.

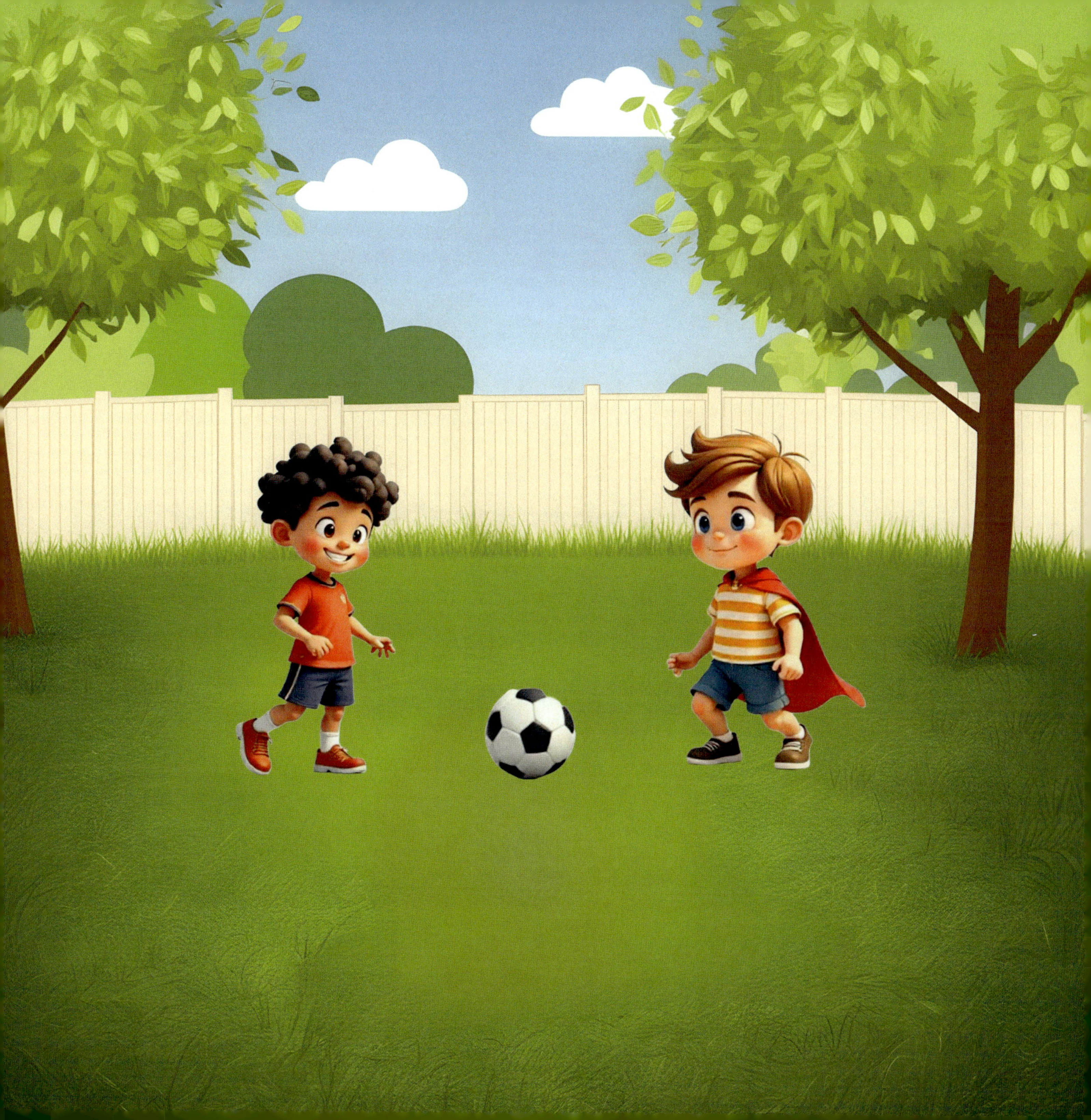

Tired from playing, Danny went inside for lunch. On his plate was a sandwich, but something was wrong it wasn't his favorite cheese! "I asked for cheddar, not this!" he thought. His stomach grumbled as he stared at the sandwich.

His fingers twitched. What should Danny do?

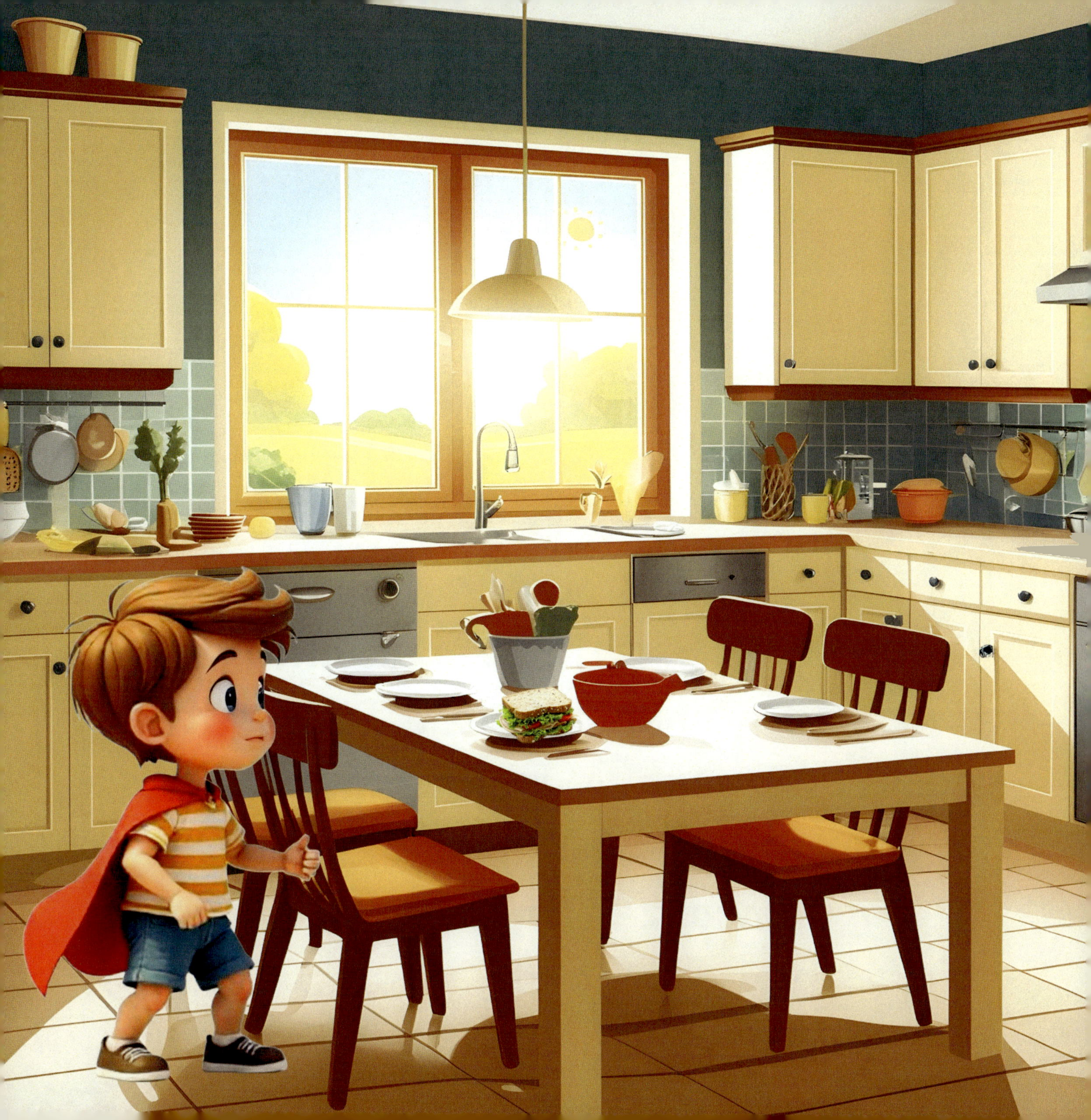

Danny had two choices:

1. Complain loudly and push the plate away.

2. Thank Mom and eat the sandwich anyway.

Danny picked up the sandwich and took a bite. "Thanks, Mom! It's pretty good," he said. Mom smiled. "I'll make your favorite next time, promise." Danny realized that heroes aren't picky they appreciate what they have.

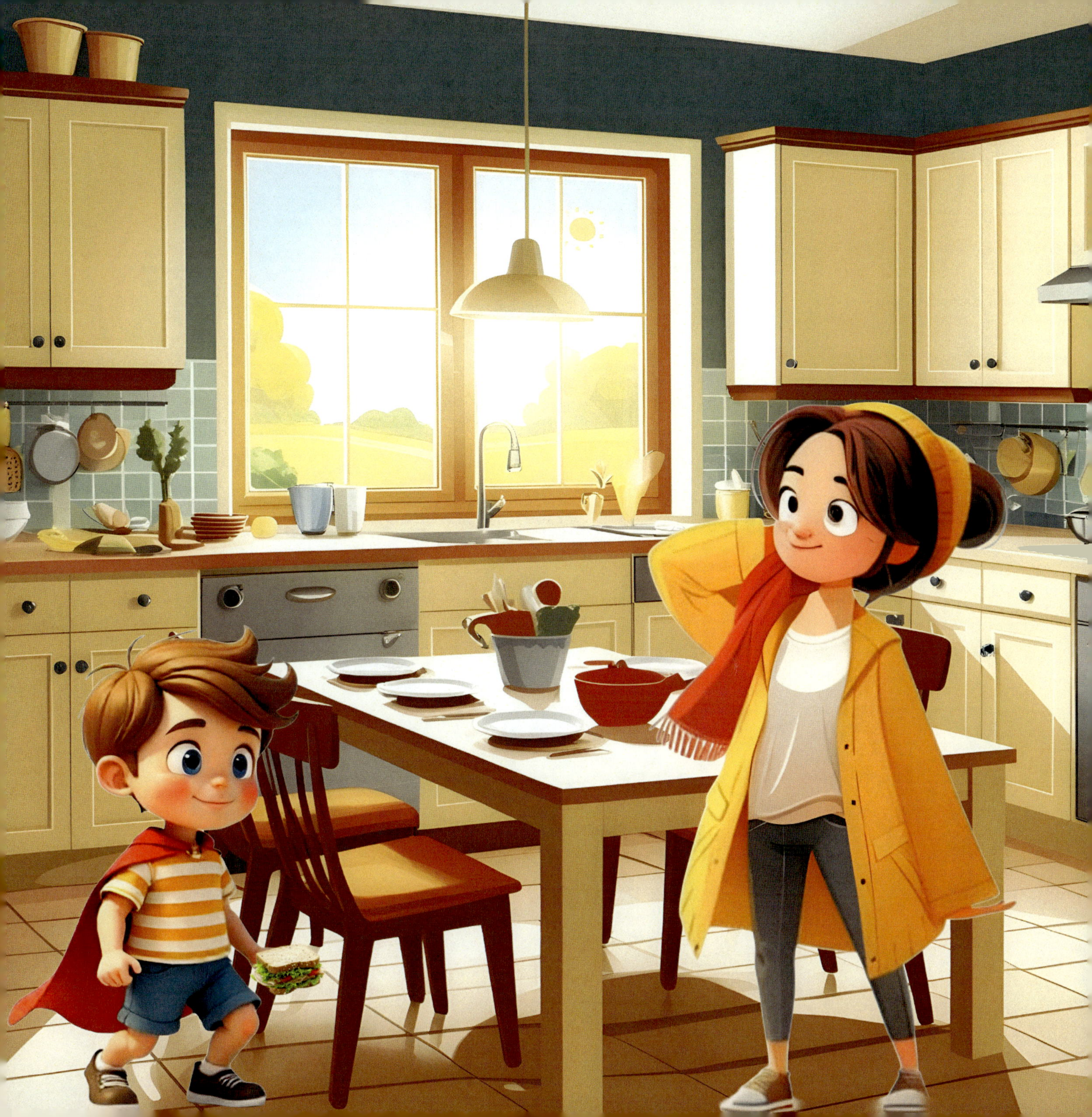

Later that afternoon, Danny's big sister, Mia, entered his room. "Can I wear your superhero cape for a bit?" she asked. Danny hesitated. The cape was his most prized possession. What if she ripped it? What if she didn't give it back?

His hands clutched the cape. What should Danny do?

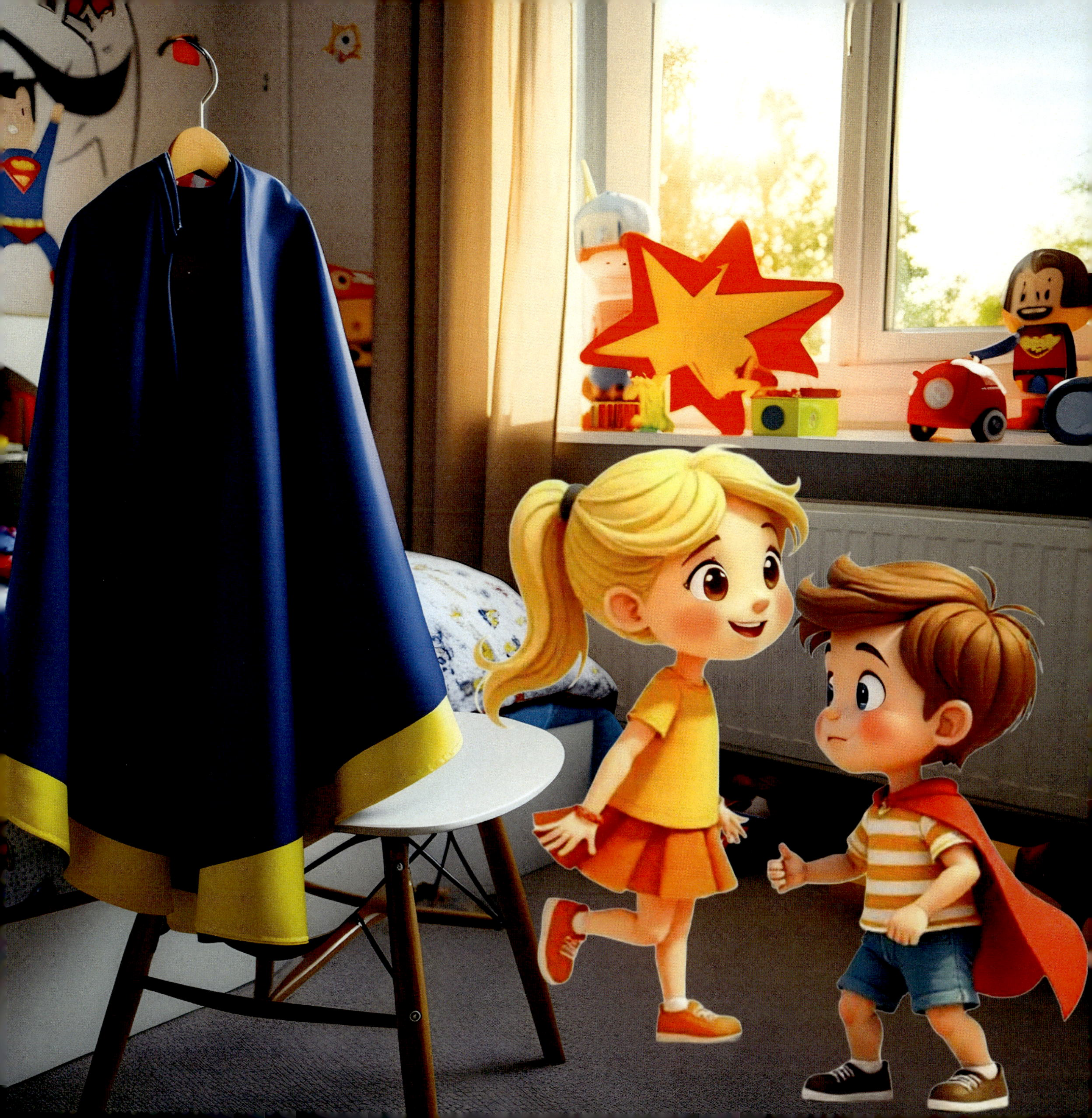

Danny had two choices:

1. Shout "No way!" and hide the cape.

2. Let Mia borrow it for a little while.

Danny sighed and handed her the cape. "Just be careful," he said. Mia twirled around, beaming. "You're the best, Danny!" she said. Watching her pretend to be a superhero, Danny felt proud. Sharing wasn't so bad after all.

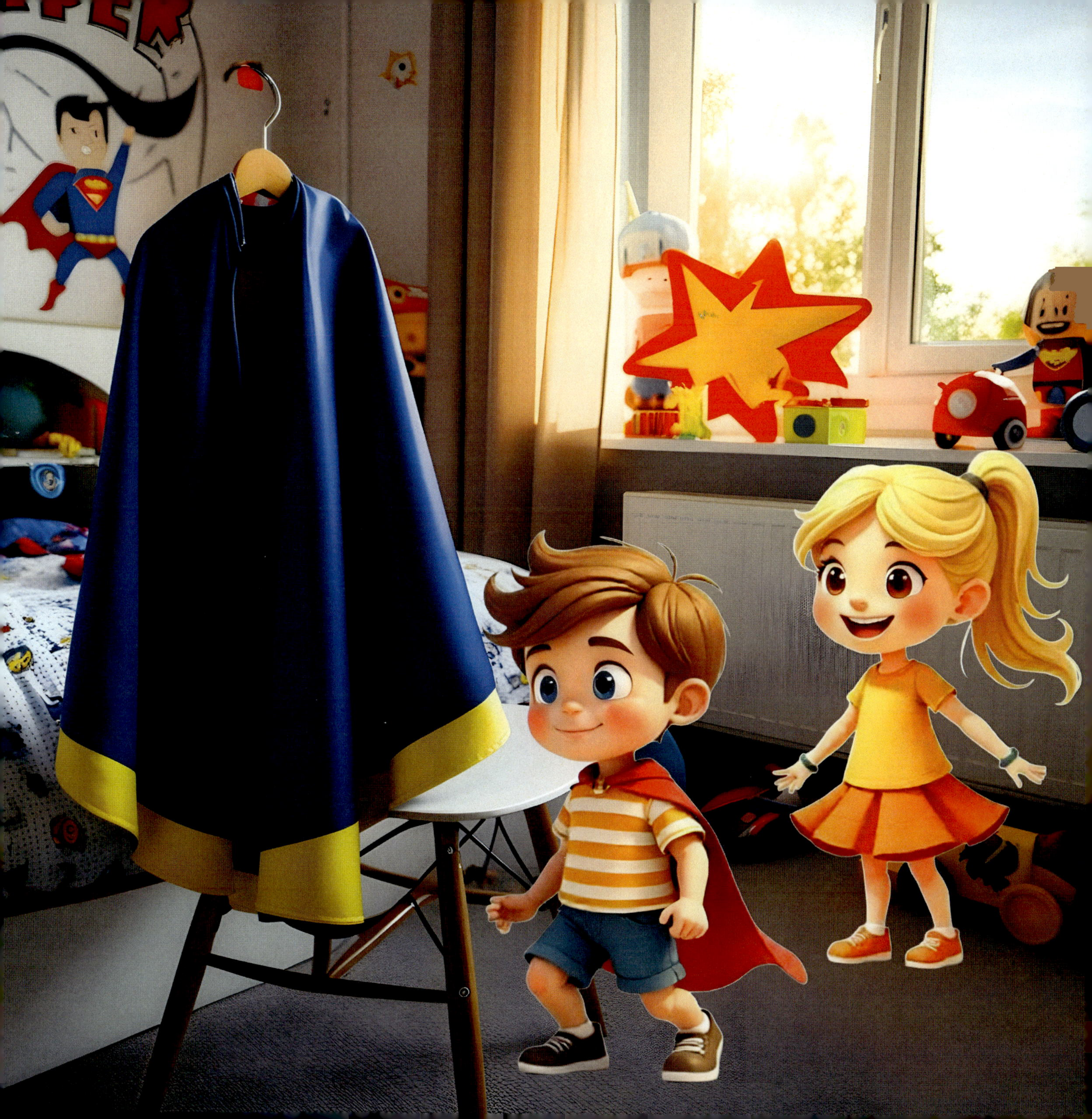

As the sun set, Danny wandered into the kitchen and spotted the cookie jar. His eyes lit up. The cookies inside smelled sweet and buttery. His mouth watered. But he remembered Mom's rule: always ask first.

His hand hovered over the jar. What should Danny do?

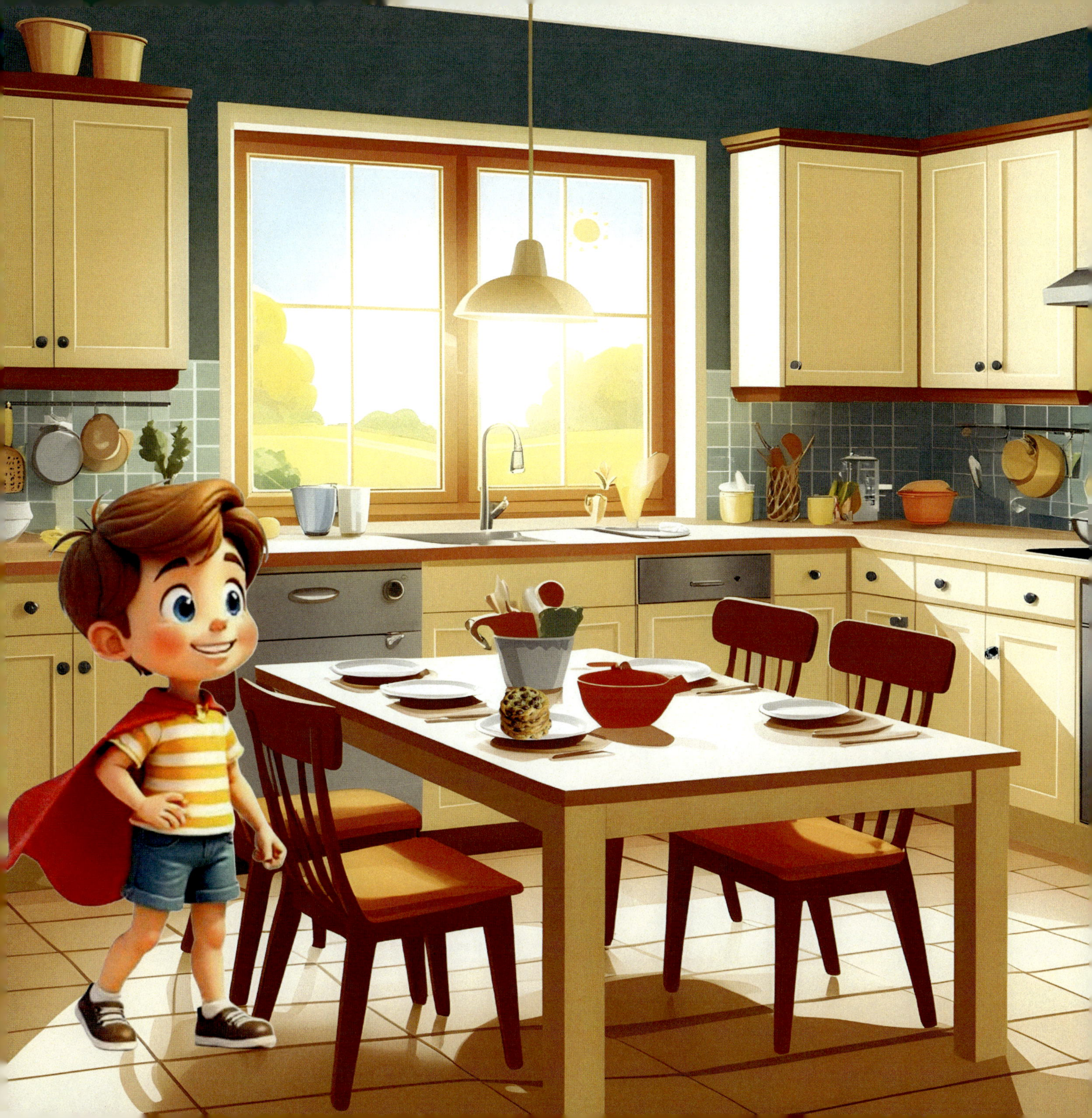

Danny had two choices:

1. Sneak a cookie and hope no one noticed.

2. Ask Mom for permission.

Danny called out, "Mom, can I have a cookie?" Mom peeked in and nodded. "Thank you for asking, Danny. Take two!" Danny grabbed the cookies and smiled. They tasted even better because he made the right choice.

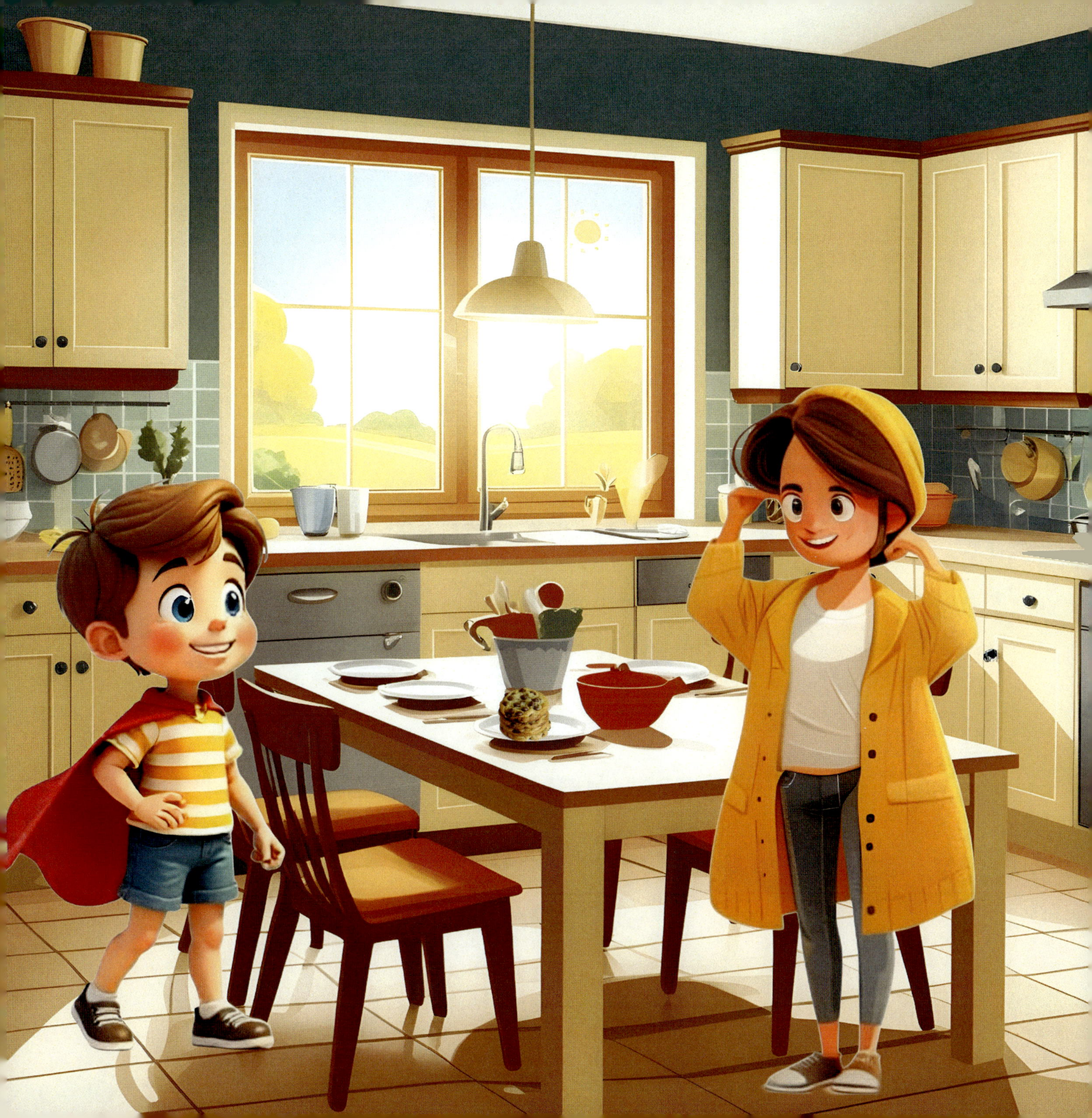

At bedtime, Dad sat beside Danny with a book about a brave knight. The knight faced dangerous dragons and made tough decisions. As Dad read, Danny thought about his day. "I think I made some pretty good choices too," he said. "Maybe I'm a superhero already!"

Dad chuckled. "You are, Danny. Every good choice you make makes you stronger."

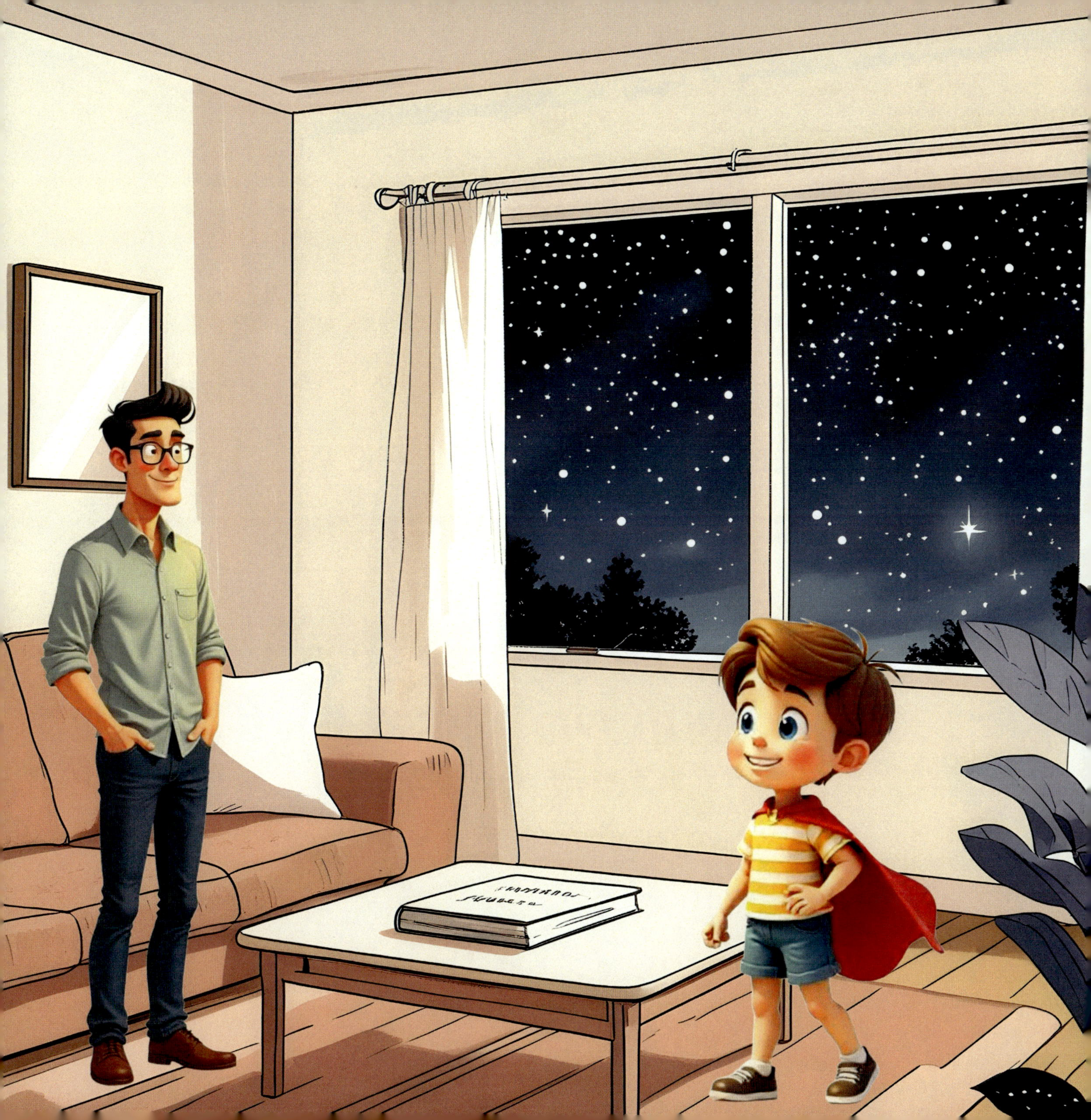

Danny snuggled under the covers as Dad kissed him goodnight. "Tomorrow's another day to be a hero," Dad whispered. Danny smiled, imagining all the new choices he'd have to make. As he drifted off to sleep, one thought stayed with him: What will I do tomorrow?

Thank You

For Choosing My Book